Economically Developing Countries

Malaysia

Jonathan Rowell

RSVP

RAINTREE
STECK-VAUGHN
P U B L I S H E R S
The Steck-Vaughn Company

Austin, Texas

Economically Developing Countries

Bangladesh

Brazil

China

Egypt

Ghana

India

Malaysia

Mexico

Nigeria

Peru

South Korea

Vietnam

Title page: Mount Kinabalu in Sabah. Breathtaking scenery like this needs to be preserved.
Contents page: A group of Malay children play together in a park.

Picture acknowledgments:
All the photographs in this book were taken by Jimmy Holmes except Allan Flachs 41,43: Ole Steen Hansen 3,4,17.
Illustrations by Peter Bull.

Published by Raintree Steck-Vaughn Publishers, an imprint of Steck-Vaughn Company

Library of Congress Cataloging-in-Publication Data
Rowell, Jonathan.
Malaysia / Jonathan Rowell.
    p.   cm.—(Economically Developing Countries)
    Includes bibliographical references and index.
    Summary: Examines the history, geography, and current economic conditions in Malaysia and discusses where the country is headed in the future.
    ISBN 0-8172-4531-6
    1. Malaysia—Economic conditions—Juvenile literature.
    2. Malaysia—Juvenile literature.
    [1. Malaysia.]
    I. Title. II. Series.
    HC445.5.R7 1997
    330.9595'054—dc20   96-17968

Printed in Italy. Bound in the United States.
1 2 3 4 5 6 7 8 9 0 01 00 99 98 97

Contents

Introduction

Malaysia is a complex country because it is made up of two parts and is divided into three separate territories. West Malaysia is a long finger of land known as the Malay Peninsula, surrounded by the South China Sea. East Malaysia consists of Sabah and Sarawak and forms a strip along the northern coast of the island of Borneo, 435 miles across the South China Sea. The eleven states of the Malay Peninsula, along with Sabah and Sarawak, form the Federation of Malaysia.

Malaysia is a country of contrasts. In East Malaysia, the indigenous peoples still live in the forests, whereas in West Malaysia modern cities are common and the people's lifestyles are similar to those of Europe or the United States.

Malaysia's position at the heart of Asia means that it lies on the major trading routes of the Asian continent. This has led to a mixed and varied population, in which ethnic Malays live alongside Chinese and Indian people as well as other indigenous peoples.

THE MALAYSIAN FLAG

The Malaysian flag has been in use since independence was gained from Great Britain in 1963. The fourteen stripes and the fourteen points on the star, which resemble the roof of the national mosque in Kuala Lumpur, represent the original fourteen Malaysian states. When Singapore left the union in 1965, the extra point and stripe were left to stand for the capital city, Kuala Lumpur. The crescent alongside the star is a sign of Islam, the official religion. The yellow is the official color of the monarchy, the blue reminds people of the influence of British colonial rule, and the red and white are Malaysia's traditional colors.

In central Kuala Lumpur new high-rise office buildings tower over old colonial buildings—a relic of Malaysia's past.

MALAYSIA AT A GLANCE

Area:	127,320 sq. mi.
Official Language:	Malay (*Bahasa Melayu*)
Population:	19.5 million
Population Density:	135 persons per sq. mi.
Capital:	Kuala Lumpur
Currency:	Malaysian Dollar, or *Ringgit*
Official Religion:	Islam
Independence Gained:	1963
Prime Minister:	Dr. Mahathir Mohammed

Source: *The Financial Times*, 1995

Above *The thirteen states of Malaysia*

- —— Main roads
- ++++++ Railroads
- ✈ International airports

Malays make up 47 percent of the population in Malaysia, and they hold a position of advantage in Malaysian society. A New Economic Policy (NEP), which was first introduced in the early 1970s, benefits Malays by helping them find work, giving them special rights to own land, and recommending that secondary education be taught in *Bahasa Melayu*, the mother tongue.

Malaysia is a rapidly developing country. It has held a position as one of the fastest-growing economies in Asia since 1988. The economy was once ruled by the production of tin, rubber, and lumber, but now manufactured goods, such as computer disk drives and cars, account for two-thirds of Malaysia's exports. In a short time, Malaysia will no longer be an economically developing country, but a newly industrialized one.

Development in Malaysia must be carefully planned if it is to continue successfully. The government, which is well supported by the people, keeps Malaysia's growth on track by setting targets to be achieved before progressing further. Full industrialization by 2020 is Malaysia's most ambitious target to date.

Opposite In Kelantan, on the Malay Peninsula, a Malay farmer returns from his workday in the rice fields. These productive flat plains contrast with the mountains inland.

SOCIAL INDICATORS OF DEVELOPMENT		
Life Expectancy	Male 69	Female 73
Infant Mortality	20 per 1,000	
Percentage of Adults who		
can Read and Write	78%	
Access to Safe Water	78%	
	Source: *World Bank Development Report, 1995*	

Below Kota Kinabalu is the state capital of Sabah, situated at the tip of East Malaysia.

1786	The British occupy Penang, an island off the north coast of Malaysia, and set up a colony ruled from India
1896	Selangor, Negeri Sembilan, and Pahang become the Federated Malay States (FMS) under the supervision of British administrator
1919	"British Malaya" formed as all the peninsula states join together
1930	Malaysian Communist Party (MCP) formed
1942	Despite the presence of British forces in World War II, British Malaya and Singapore are occupied by the Japanese
1948	British establish Federation of Malaya—an expansion of the FMS, including Pinang and Malacca. A communist insurrection begins and lasts until 1960, spurring the movement for independence
1957	Malaya achieves independence (*merdeka*). First Prime Minister Tengku Abdul Rahman appointed
1963	Singapore, Sabah, and Sarawak join Malaya to form the Federation of Malaysia
1965	Singapore and Malaysia separate. As most of the population of Singapore were Chinese, they did not want to be ruled by Malays. Malays also feared the influence of Singapore because of its high Chinese population
1981	Dr. Mahathir Mohammed becomes Malaysia's fourth Prime Minister and still holds that office

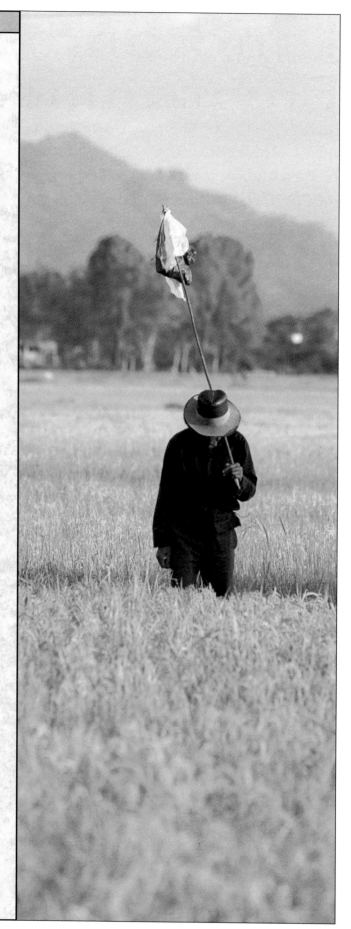

Land and the Environment

WEST MALAYSIA

In West Malaysia, a central chain of mountains divides the country into its geographical regions. The mountains separate fertile lowlands to the west from a narrow belt on the eastern coast. Human activity on the western plains has transformed the landscape. Both the rural areas and the towns and cities are heavily populated. There are many Malay villages surrounded by rice fields. Rubber and oil palm plantations alongside tin mines help to make this an industrial zone. The population is a mixture of Malay, Chinese, and Indian peoples.

East and south of the mountains, the second lowland region has a different character. This area is less developed, poorer, more rural, and less densely populated. The majority of people living in this area are Malays, whose activities are based upon small-scale farming and fishing.

Few people live in the mountains because the summits are outcrops of bare rock, usually limestone, and the slopes are cloaked in dense vegetation that is difficult to penetrate.

In the hot climate, clouds rise above the thick, mountainous forests following an afternoon rainstorm.

West Malaysia is divided geographically by a central chain of mountains. Lowland regions to the west are heavily populated. In East Malaysia, coastal plains rise into the mountains bordering Indonesia.

Kota Bahru

Kuala Lumpur

Johor Bahru

Mount Kinabalu

Kota Kinabalu

Kuching

N

| 0 | 100 | 200 | 300 | 400 | 500 km |
| 0 | | 100 | | 200 | 300 miles |

Malaysia accounts for more than half the world's exports of tropical lumber compared with 26.7 percent from Indonesia and 2.4 percent from Brazil.

In the past, the small population of forest people cleared trees to plant their crops. However, they moved often and left the cleared areas to regrow for long periods.

Logging today is not the same sustainable process. Tropical lumber is a valuable resource. To supply the developed world's demand for lumber, a huge rise in commercial logging has taken place. Because the demand is so high, there is no time to let the old forests regrow and instead they are replaced by fast-growing trees that damage the soils. The complex root systems of the old forest trees are gone, which means they no longer hold the soil together. Once the soil is washed away, the old forests can never grow again on this land.

Today, the future of tropical logging is threatened not only by competition from cooler climates but also by the possibility that the lumber may eventually run out.

"My husband drives a truck like this, which takes logs from the interior of Sabah through to the sawmill. He is often away for weeks at a time and we never get a chance to see him, so we came out here to visit. We are quite lucky though because this is a good job and he is well paid. We live in the town in our own house with the luxuries that we want."
— **Winnie Chan (logger's wife)**

EAST MALAYSIA

In East Malaysia, the coastal plains are characterized by mangrove swamps that rise into mountains on the border with Indonesia. Flowing across the states to the coast are large rivers, such as the Rajang River in Sarawak and the Kinabatangan River in Sabah. In East Malaysia, the water has worn away the rock, and huge caves have appeared. Cave systems at Niah and Mulu in Sarawak are still being discovered, and some, such as the Sarawak Chamber, are the biggest in the world. In Sabah, Mount Kinabalu is the highest mountain between the Himalayas and New Guinea.

Logging means that Winnie, pictured here with her daughter, can live in a way she might never have dreamed of when she was young.

9

The Endau Rompin National Park

Although 2,880 square miles of forest in Malaysia is protected, there has been only one national park, the Taman Negara, situated on the Malay Peninsula. To protect more land, the government chose to conserve the Endau Rompin forest, which covers the border between the states of Johor and Pahang, because it was an undisturbed stretch of forest.

There was already a wildlife sanctuary on the Johor side, which protected the endangered Sumatran Rhinoceros among many other animal species. The original idea was to preserve 780 square miles of land. The area was to include a fully protected core of 355 square miles, and the remaining 425 square miles was going to be managed as a forest reserve. However, in 1977, it became known that the Pahang state government had approved plans to log 46 square miles of the core area and the logging had already begun. The Malaysian people protested, and the state finally gave in, refusing to issue any more logging licenses. However, 20 square miles of forest had already been cleared.

In 1980, a National Parks Act was passed, which meant that Endau Rompin achieved full status as a conservation area. However, the state of Pahang refused to hand over the land to the Malaysian government.

An angry public, helped by the Malayan Nature Society, continued to press for change. Finally, in 1988, Endau Rompin became a park without the state's losing control of its land. Although the park protects a smaller area than was originally hoped for (359 square miles rather than 780 square miles), it remains a victory for conservationists.

East Malaysia is less developed than the Malay Peninsula. There are few towns, and the infrastructure is just beginning to expand. Great emphasis is placed on primary production such as agriculture, lumber, and oil. Despite its isolation (it takes two and a half hours to fly from Kuala Lumpur in West Malaysia to Kota Kinabalu in Sabah), East Malaysia is of great economic importance to the whole of the country.

The Kinabatangan River in Sabah

The clouds before the storm are a daily sight in many parts of Malaysia.

CLIMATE

The tropical climate of Malaysia is characterized by high temperatures and humidity year-round. It rains from 150 to 200 days out of the year, but the rain rarely lasts all of each day. In West Malaysia, the wet season occurs on the west coast from September to December and on the east coast, where it is more pronounced, between October and February. In East Malaysia, the rain is even heavier, and flooding is common.

Temperatures rarely fall below 68°F even at night and usually climb to 85°F or higher during the day.

CLIMATE			
KUALA LUMPUR		**LABUAN, SABAH**	
Month	Average rainfall (in.)	Month	Average rainfall (in.)
Jan	6	Jan	4
Feb	8	Feb	5
March	10	March	6
April	12	April	12
May	9	May	14
June	5	June	14
July	4	July	13
Aug	7	Aug	11
Sept	9	Sept	17
Oct	10	Oct	19
Nov	10	Nov	17
Dec	8	Dec	11
Source: World Weather Guide, 1990			

FLORA AND FAUNA

Examples of some of the most ancient forests in the world can be found in Malaysia. It is home to one of the most varied plant communities in existence and an enormous number of animal species. More than 2,000 types of trees and 200 kinds of palms have been recorded, and in the canopy high above the forest floor many insects remain unidentified. Some of the most bizarre insects disguise themselves as natural objects, such as branches or flowers. On Mount Kinabalu, the slopes are covered by almost 1,000 orchids and pitcher plants, so called because their leaves form sacks that can hold liquids to trap insects. The world's largest flower, rafflesia, originated in Sabah. The rafflesia blooms quickly and is rarely spotted, which is surprising because the flower can grow to 10 feet in width. Despite its beauty, the rafflesia smells of rotting meat to attract flies that will pollinate the flower before it rapidly withers.

The rain forest, however, is under threat from logging. Lumber production is vital to the Malaysian economy, so the felling of trees to be cut into logs continues. This results in the deforestation of large areas. To protect the environment, a balance between logging rights and conservation has been struck. In 1935, the Taman Negara National Park was created. A smaller area than ever has been set aside for tree clearance, and many trees have been replanted in zones that have already been cleared. However, the actual area of forest available for logging has already been dramatically reduced.

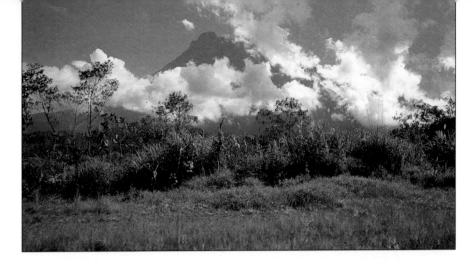

Clouds in Sabah surround the summit of Mount Kinabalu, which is 13,432 ft. high.

Convoys of logging trucks are common on Malaysian roads.

No one is certain where the name Kinabalu comes from. It may be derived from *Aki Nabalu* meaning "sacred place of the dead" in the local dialect, Dusun. But the indigenous peoples, the Kadazan, have another explanation. An emperor of China had heard that the mountain was home to a fabulous pearl and sent his three sons to find it and bring it back to him. The mountain was protected by a dragon, who drove the first two sons away. While they made their escape, the third son managed to snatch the jewel, but decided to remain in Borneo. He married and, after raising a family, chose to return to China to take his place on the throne. He promised that he would come back for his wife, but he never did. So, in despair, she decided to climb the mountain to pray that he would come back for her. However, she died before she reached the summit of the mountain, so the Kadazan believe that Mount Kinabalu was named after her because *Kina* means "China" and *balu* means "widow."

Yassan Sekambeng explains the importance of preserving scenic places such as Mount Kinabalu.

"For over ten years I have been working on this mountain. This place means a lot to me, although it does not mean the same to me as it does to my parents. My folks used to think that the mountain had a spirit, and that we would go there when we died. But to me, it has a more realistic meaning. Many guides and porters earn a living by working with the tourists here. We enjoy our work and respect the wildlife and forest. But more people have to learn that we must preserve these special places."
—Yassan Sekambeng, Kinabalu mountain guide

13

Transportation

In Malaysia, much has been done to improve the communications network. A good communications network by road, rail, air, and water is essential to the development of any country, but the geography of Malaysia, with its central mountain ranges, makes it a difficult task.

ROADS

In Malaysia, many roads began as logging tracks, or routes that led to rubber plantations and tin mines. Now these have been upgraded, lengthened, and joined to form a modern transportation network. The road system of any country is a good marker of its development, and where there are roads, the local districts can grow. Roads are concentrated mainly in the industrialized western region. Here, the north-south highway from Butterworth to Johor Bahru, via Kuala Lumpur, links the main towns.

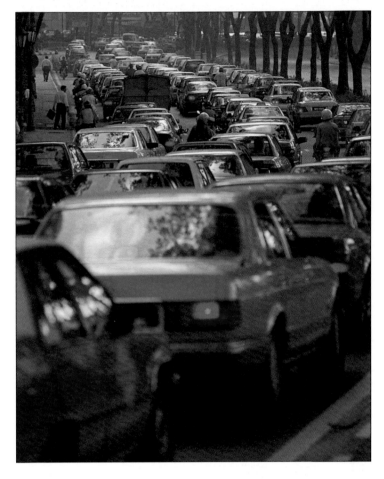

Above A traffic jam during the rush hour in Kuala Lumpur. This scene is repeated in all Malaysia's major towns.

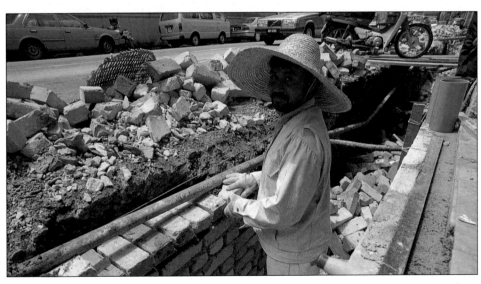

Left A road worker repairs a drain at the side of a modern city road.

As the road network has expanded, more remote states have become easier to reach. A 4-mile-long bridge now links Penang to the mainland, and this has helped the island to attract industry. Even the central mountain chain in West Malaysia has been crossed. In the far north, close to the Thai border, a winding road joins the west and east coasts. It is now paved along its entire length and has improved access to the traditional state of Kelantan, where strict Islamic law is observed, alcohol is banned, and women are often veiled.

Sabah is the best example in Malaysia of how the rate of development depends on communications. In 1985, roads between the major towns were still mostly dirt tracks. By 1995, all routes even as far as Tawau in the southeast were paved, making journeys shorter and more comfortable. As a consequence, in the same ten-year period, the number of people owning cars tripled.

The main north–south highway on the Malay Peninsula is a divided highway for much of its length.

To avoid congestion, which slows traffic during peak hours to a walking pace, a new Light Rapid Transit System (LRT) has opened in Kuala Lumpur. The system operates electric trains and has been running since August 1995.

A train operator on Kuala Lumpur's new LRT prepares for his trip to the suburbs.

The first reactions of Kuala Lumpur's residents were mixed. For the first few days, all rides were free and the system was well used. But some still complained because it did not go near enough to their houses; others said they could not afford the proposed fares. Indeed, the number of people traveling on the service dropped once fares were charged. So, many were using it only because it was free. However, others continued to use and to pay for the new trains. They enjoyed the added comfort and speed of the service. Some said they would leave their cars at home and were looking forward to the growth of the service.

"The new rolling stock of the railway has really changed the way people think about the train system. I've seen so many people start to commute by train and leave their cars at home. It's so much more efficient. The roads are so busy these days, with long traffic jams, and it's expensive to find a place to park in the city. As soon as the new LRT elevated train system is completed the situation will get even better." —**LRT train operator**

Below *Parts of central Kuala Lumpur are so congested that tracks for new trains have been built above the roads.*

RAILROADS

Like the original road network, the railroads were first built in colonial times. The main railroad line runs north–south through the western region of the Malay Peninsula.

A secondary line links Kota Bahru in the northeast of West Malaysia to Kuala Lumpur and passes through the middle of the central mountain chain where there are no roads. Small-scale industry and some settlements have appeared along the route of this so-called Jungle Railway.

The new Light Rapid Transit System (LRT), linking Kuala Lumpur and its suburbs, started operating services in the summer of 1995. It was built to ease congestion on the city's roads.

AIR AND WATER TRANSPORTION

Even though Malaysia is not a big country, it will always be difficult and time consuming to reach parts of it by land. The problem is overcome by using other forms of transportation. A reliable air service has been introduced, and most settlements larger than a village have an airstrip. Malaysian Airlines provides daily flights between most towns and cities.

A Boeing 737 ready for takeoff. Malaysia has the biggest fleet in Asia.

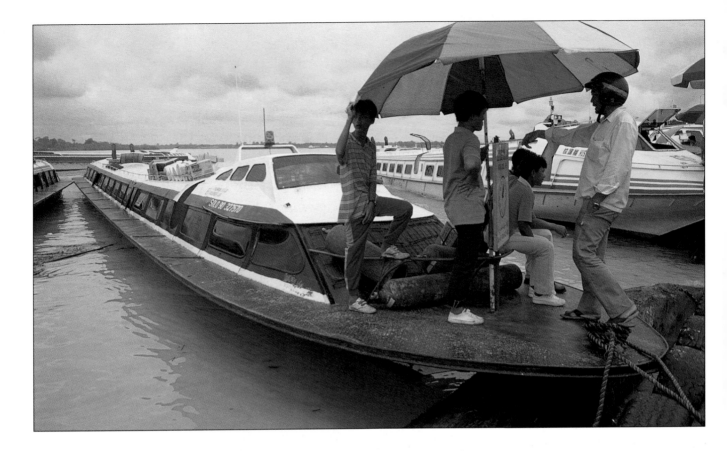

At smaller locations you can expect to disembark from a small aircraft onto a runway with all your belongings and cargo. This contrasts sharply with the international airport, Subang, which is modern, air-conditioned, and spacious. As a mark of Malaysia's worldwide reputation, Subang has become overcrowded and is being replaced by a new airport at Sepang.

In some places rivers offer the only practical means of communication. In Sarawak, for example, the people are dependent on river transportation. Inland waterways are navigable deep into the interior. Fast launches, called *expres,* which can travel 35 to 40 mph, ferry goods and passengers to markets farther downstream or on the coast.

For a country surrounded by water, marine transport is very important. As the number of foreign markets supplied by Malaysian products grows, the freight coming in and going out of Malaysia increases. To deal with this extra trade, international ports such as those at Melaka and Butterworth are constantly developing.

A crew at Sibu wait for cargo, which their fast launch will carry upriver into the interior of Sarawak.

The Many Peoples of Malaysia

Malaysian society is characterized by the diversity of its ethnic groups and its location at the center of trading routes between India and China. Malaysia's peoples include Malay, Chinese, Tamil (Indian), and indigenous groups. In West Malaysia, indigenous groups are referred to as *Orang Asli*, and in East Malaysia, *Dayaks*.

The most important distinction in Malaysian society is between the Muslim Malays and the Chinese. Although the Malays are the largest group, they amount to only about 55 percent of the total population in West Malaysia, and even less in East Malaysia. Malays are called *bumiputera*. They choose Islam as their only religion and follow Malay culture in all its forms. Their official language, *Bahasa Melayu*, is also the official national language and is spoken in Malaysian business and education. Malays are generally country people rather than town people.

For the Chinese, the coffee shop is more than just somewhere to eat and drink, it is also a place to socialize and to read the paper.

"The Chinese community has been in the Taiping area of Malaysia for over 150 years. We came here originally to work the tin mines and do laboring jobs. We have our traditions still, and this old-style coffee shop has changed little over the years."
—Mr. Ho Kok Liong, Chinese coffee shop customer

19

As Malaysia's industry has grown, the number of people moving to cities to find jobs and to improve their standards of living has increased. When industry stopped growing, during the recession of the early 1980s, for example, the movement to towns slowed because there were fewer new jobs. People have always been attracted to big cities.

To prevent the overcrowding that this leads to, the Malaysian government has encouraged the development of smaller towns in Kelantan, Kedah, Perlis, and Pahang. As this has not stopped the flow of people to the largest cities, such as Kuala Lumpur, new settlements have been built on the edges of these areas. Services and work are provided locally to keep people away from the center. Over the past twenty years, more than fifty new towns have been planned or are being developed.

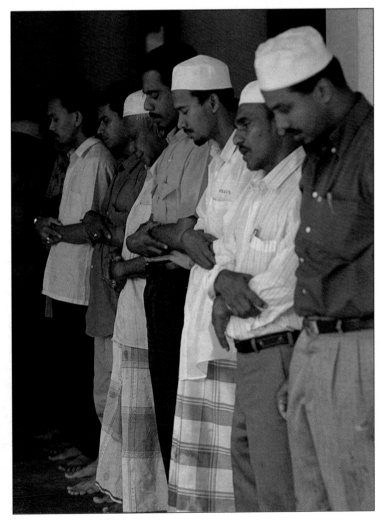

Although there were Chinese people in Malaysia from early times, their numbers greatly increased during the nineteenth century.

Most came from the southern provinces of China and now make up 32 percent of the population of Malaysia. Hakkas, Hokkiens, Teochews, and Cantonese are some of the many dialects spoken.

The Chinese have kept their religious and cultural practices and rarely spend any time socially with people who are not Chinese. Most Chinese people live in towns and cities, where they control the majority of businesses.

Islam is the national religion of Malaysia. Malay men pray at a mosque.

"My father moved here to Malaysia when I was still young. I suppose he was looking for a better life and followed my other relatives who had been in Malaysia for some time. Business is good here, and there are plenty of business opportunities in such a rapidly growing economy. Things are changing so quickly here now."
—**Miss Thavaman, Indian trader**

Many Indians in Malaysia are merchants. An Indian storekeeper displays the materials she sells.

The third major group, the Indians, account for 8 percent of the population. They came to work on the plantations for British colonists around the beginning of the twentieth century. They are mainly Tamils and now live in the larger towns on the west coast of West Malaysia.

Small and scattered indigenous groups together make up 12 percent of the population. In West Malaysia, the *Orang Asli*, the "Original People," consist of three main groups—Negritos, Senoi, and Jakun. Living mainly in the mountains, they work as farmers or collect forest products. Traditional shifting cultivation has been abandoned as they have become more integrated into Malay society.

In East Malaysia, the mix of non-Muslim peoples is more complicated. Together, the ethnic groups are called *Dayaks*, but they consist of more than 200 different groups. In Sarawak, the Iban is the most common, followed by the Bidayuh. The majority live in communal dwellings called longhouses, which are built on the banks of the great rivers. These people are directly affected by deforestation because their way of life depends on the habitat that is being destroyed. The Penan suffer most because they continue to live a hunter-gatherer existence.

ETHNIC AND RELIGIOUS DIVERSITY IN MALAYSIA

ETHNIC DIVISION	Percentage of population
Malay	47%
Chinese	29%
Indigenous groups	12%
Indian	8%
Other	4%

RELIGIONS	Percentage of population
Islam	53%
Buddhist	17%
Chinese Faiths	12%
Hindu	7%
Christian	6%
Other	5%

Source: The World of Figures: *The Economist*, 1987

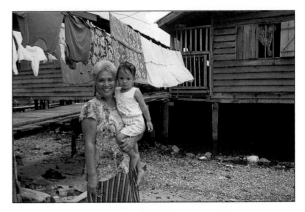

"I'm from the Philippines originally, but we've lived in Sandakan, almost in this exact spot, for over twenty years now. I wouldn't live anywhere else. We have such a great community spirit, and such a mixed bunch of folks. Indonesians, Malays, Chinese, and we all get along together."
—Aida Javines, inhabitant of a stilt house

In Sabah, Kadazans form the major ethnic group, alongside the Murat and Sulu. Traditionally, the Kadazan are farmers, but many have now moved to the towns to find work. In the past, the Sulu people were known to be pirates. However, it is now thought to be illegal

Stilt houses provide accommodations for the many immigrants in Sabah.

The Impact of Development on Indigenous Groups of Sarawak

"We aren't quite sure who is cutting our forests and who is going to flood our land. But we know they live in towns, where rich people are getting richer while we poor people are losing what little we have."
—Iban statement

Sibu, 37 miles from the mouth of the Rajang River in Sarawak, is a point where traditional and modern worlds meet. It is a Chinese town, where boats on the wide river compete for trade. The streets are peopled by *Dayak*s, particularly the Iban, who can be identified by their elaborate tattoos. In years gone by, the Iban would not have traveled this far, but many have been forced off their land

by development projects. Now they come to towns such as Sibu to find work. Other indigenous groups pass through Sibu on their way to Kuching, the capital of Sarawak. They hope to find tourists who want to visit and stay in a *Dayak* longhouse. Tourist trips to longhouses are set to become a major source of income for communities who live in this traditional way.

The different indigenous groups have never lived entirely without contact with one another or the outside world. They would meet to trade or to fight wars, but they remained independent and self-sufficient. The people exploited the rain forest with an economy based on shifting cultivation. They ate root

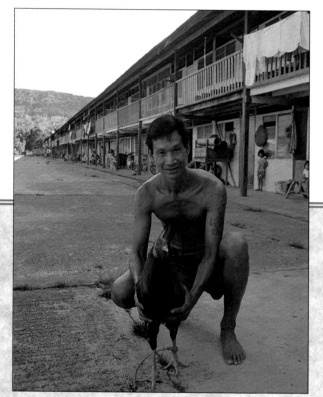

immigrants from the Philippines or Indonesia who are responsible. They live in the coastal towns of Sandakan, Lahad Datu, and Tawau.

Even though there is a great variety of peoples in Malaysia, the country is underpopulated. Unlike elsewhere in the world, where overpopulation is often the reason for the slow pace of development, the Malaysian economy will not continue to grow without an increase in the number of people. People are the fuel that help economies to grow. Without enough people to fill the jobs in an increasingly expanding economy, growth will stop.

crops and sago (starch made from the pith of the sago palm) and, where soils were suitable, cultivated wet rice.

This traditional way of life is, however, slowly being destroyed. That is because the forests are ideal locations for hydroelectric power projects and because their timber is vital for the economy of Malaysia. These activities use land to which the Dayaks have always had access, and suitable protected areas are not being set aside for the tribes.

"We are all from the Iban ethnic group here, and this is our traditional way to live. Sharing one long building helps us stay together as a community. The materials and construction of our longhouse are new because we had to move from the valley, which is now under water after they built the hydroelectric dam." —**Nyambar Nyelang, in front of his longhouse**

For the indigenous peoples, who continue to live in the remote regions, signs of the influence of change are everywhere. The longhouse may well have been built using ancient methods, but now banks of televisions line the inside. They have electricity to turn on the sets, but the TV signal was never set up to reach that far, so when the television is switched on, the screen remains blank.

Agriculture and Natural Resources

Malaysia is blessed with many natural resources that have helped the country to develop. They fall into three basic categories—agricultural, mineral, and energy.

AGRICULTURE

The agricultural sector was once the main source of Malaysia's growth, but, as the economy and industry have grown, it has become less important. However, its decline is partly due to the kind of agriculture that is practiced.

Over the past twenty years, government policy has favored small farms. The farmers of these small agricultural areas own and live on the land. Despite the fact that this is not an economical way to farm, Malays were encouraged to stay on the land with financial aid from the government. The government aimed to help the poor by giving Malays a greater share of the country's wealth, but it was not an efficient way to get the best from the land. At times, for example, Malay farmers would spend more money growing cash

When sections of forest are cleared, they are often replaced by large plantations.

TRADE IN COMMODITIES				
COMMODITY	1950	1970	1980	1990
Palm oil (tons)	54,000	500,000	2,800,000	6,820,000
Palm kernels (tons)	12,000	104,000	594,000	1,738,000
Rubber (tons)	794,000	1,384,000	1,762,000	1,562,000
Sawlogs (million cubic feet)	455.5	851.4	1,197	1,412.9
Tin (feet)	165,682	296,260	233,924	91,864

Sources: *Philips Geographical Digest*, 1992–93
Economist Intelligence Unit Country Profile: Malaysia and Brunei, 1995–96

An oil palm plantation in Sabah, East Malaysia. Oil palm plantations cover huge areas of land.

crops, such as rubber, oil palm, or cocoa, than they would make when their produce was sold. Discouraged by the small amounts of money that they were getting back from their investment, farmers grew rice, vegetables, or tropical fruits instead. With these crops they could at least feed their families, and any that was left over could be sold at the local market.

Many decided that farming had become too much of a risk and left the countryside altogether. They moved to towns to work in jobs that offered more security and better pay. In response, the government supported a return to large-scale farming. Large plantations could buy machinery and fertilizers that small farmers could never afford. They made more money because cash crops are better suited to large-scale production. Overall, costs were also reduced by replacing the many workers with machinery. This helped to protect the plantation owners financially when prices for agricultural produce were low. After all, salaries did not have to be paid to the machines.

The Palm Oil Industry

The lasting memories of many who visit Malaysia are the bitter smells as they drive through the countryside, the furry, pine conelike objects they swerve to avoid in the road, and smoke billowing from the middle of a plantation. These are all due to Malaysia's most important agricultural product, palm oil. Crude palm oil (CPO) is pressed from the fleshy outer part of a palm fruit. These fruits grow in bunches of between 800 and 1,000. Two years after they have reached the plantation, the oil palms begin producing enough oil to sell commercially. The oil from the palm can be harvested for about thirty years, after which the tree becomes too tall. Each tree will produce between five and fifteen bunches of palm fruit per year; the average yield is about 4 tons of fruit for every two and one-half acres.

Once harvested, the fruit must be ground rapidly because it deteriorates quickly. Palm oil mills are always located on or near a plantation. They produce CPO, which can then be refined further to make industrial products, such as soap, or foodstuffs, such as cooking oil. Palm fruits also produce palm kernels from which palm kernel oil is extracted. This oil is very different from CPO and is classed as a different product.

Palm oil fruit arrives at the mill on a plantation in Sabah.

The success or failure of a crop depends on its selling price and the cost of growing it. Malaysia was once the world's leading natural rubber producer, but has recently been overtaken by Thailand and Indonesia. It costs less to produce rubber in these countries because machinery is cheaper and labor costs are lower. The agricultural sector has responded in several ways. Most local workers have moved to towns, so foreign workers are employed instead—up to 70 percent on some plantations. Owners have converted their lands to produce better-paying crops. Palm oil is a

In addition, the sap of the tree can be fermented to make alcohol. So the bitter smells and the billowing smoke seem a small price to pay for such a diverse and profitable plant.

The success of palm oil can be traced to the 1950s. Malaysia's economic dependence on rubber began to decline as plantation owners looked for another crop to replace it. The infrastructure for planting large crops already existed on rubber plantations and the government allowed grants for replanting palm fruits instead. As palm oil made more money, it expanded rapidly, and Malaysia is now the world's largest producer. However, it faces stiff competition from the neighboring countries of Indonesia and Thailand, but Malaysia has found new markets, such as China, which help protect its number one position.

"There is no dispute really. Palm oil is a very successful crop. It's amazing just how many everyday products our oil goes into. It is possible that in the future we may even be able to use palm oil in motor engines. With a steady price and increasing demand, the future looks good, and we have so much empty land out here that can be planted with palms."—**Mr. Chong Min Sang, plantation manager**

A plantation manager checks the palm oil fruit after harvesting.

favorite because its market price remains high. Many owners have even sold their properties for building and leisure development.

Emphasis has also been placed on diversification and branching out into refined products that are related to agriculture. Palm oil, for instance, which was once just sold in its raw state, is now being refined and sold as oils and fats. The rubber sector has also expanded and now makes gloves and condoms.

Even though the importance of agriculture in the economy is declining, this area still employs 18.4 percent of Malaysian workers.

MINERALS

Tin was once the most important part of the Malaysian economy. The country was renowned for this raw material. In 1983, Malaysia was producing more than 660,000 tons of tin each year. Ten years later, extraction fell below 11,000 tons. Whether or not tin is mined depends on the international market price. In 1983, the metal was fetching from $5.00 to $8.00 per pound on the Kuala Lumpur tin market. In 1993, it was down to $1.70. Low prices have forced mines such as the Sungai Lembing—once one of the world's biggest single sources of tin—to be abandoned and reopened several times during the twentieth century. At the moment, the mine is still extracting ore, but only in amounts that cover the costs of keeping the mine in a workable state.

An old tin mine in Malaysia. In the years since tin was last extracted, vegetation has begun to grow over the mine.

ENERGY

In 1992, a power cut in West Malaysia left the peninsula without electricity for several days; industrial growth had caused the demand for energy to become greater than the amount being produced. The government immediately began a program to increase its energy production. To speed the process and find the money to finance the improvements, part of the national electricity board, Tenaga Nasional Berhad (TNB), was sold to the private sector. It became the largest company on the Kuala Lumpur Stock Exchange.

Independent energy producers are now building gas-fueled power stations. They will buy gas from the state-owned oil and gas company, Petronas, and sell the power to TNB. TNB is now responsible for transmitting and supplying electricity via the national grid, which is the network of power lines that run between the major power stations.

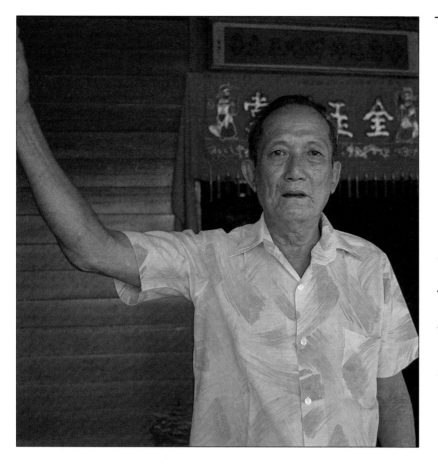

"I was born in 1935, and the big tin mines around Taiping closed in the 1950s. My father came here from Thailand to work in the mines about 1888. Now the industry is almost dead. Most of the mines have even been filled in now, and houses and shops built on the land."
—Lim-Chene Hoon, tin miner

A former tin miner remembers how important tin was once to Malaysia.

THE IMPACT OF THE OIL INDUSTRY IN KERTEH

Before the arrival of the state-owned oil company, Petronas, Kerteh was a small fishing village on the east coast of West Malaysia. Petronas is exploiting the oil offshore, and at night where Kerteh used to be dark and quiet, it is now brightly lit and buzzing with activity. The area is now characterized by its industrial skyline, and these dramatic changes have had an impact on the population. As a result, two different communities have developed: migrant employees of Petronas, who live in modern housing developments provided by the company and the locals, who still live in their traditional homes. The petroleum people care little about the area in which they live, and the locals are unsure of what the future holds.

Malaysia has the resources to be self-sufficient in energy. It has oil and gas reserves off the eastern coast of the peninsula and in the states of Sarawak and Sabah. The generation of hydroelectric power (HEP) is also becoming more important as Malaysia looks for other ways of supplying power. However, HEP projects have caused arguments and disruption. Indigenous groups are moved off land where they have lived for centuries, and the reservoirs flood areas that might be put to better use. However, such projects could make up the lack of power, or even lead to Malaysia's having a surplus of electricity.

The Bakun Dam

In the heart of the Sarawak jungle, construction on a dam powered by hydroelectricity is just beginning. The Bakun Dam will be the third largest in Asia. Almost 270 sq. mi. of prime forest will be flooded, and 6,000 people, mainly from the Penan and Kenyah peoples, will have to be moved. But the power this dam project will generate—2,400 megawatts—is not for Sarawak, but West Malaysia.

The electricity will be transmitted via 400 miles of overhead cables in Sarawak and then through 375 miles of cable beneath the South China Sea. It will be the longest underwater cable ever laid. In the process, up to 25 percent of the power may be lost. When complete, the dam will stretch 670 feet across the Rajang River.

Faced with environmental concerns, the first plans were scrapped in 1990. However, because the country needs the energy to sustain its industrial growth, the plans were recently revived.

Controversy surrounds both the study of the environmental impact that the project will cause and the dam itself. The project has now been divided into three phases: the building of a reservoir (phase 1); the building of the dam (phase 2); and the laying of the cable (phase 3). Phase 1 has been approved, but phases 2 and 3 have yet to be accepted. Breaking the study into phases has made it possible to start felling trees.

Some people welcome the project because it is expected that the dam will create new roads, new jobs, and improved opportunities and communications. For example, the town of Belaga, just below the site, can be reached only by a twice-weekly flight or seven-hour boat trip at present. However, the suggestion of chains of smaller dams, rather than a single large dam, is favored.

A small dam in Sarawak. This dam will be dwarfed by the vast Bakun Dam once it is completed.

A Developing Economy

Malaysia's economy is characterized by the exceptional growth of its manufacturing industries, the growing status of its financial markets, and the amount of construction that is taking place.

MANUFACTURING

From 1976 to 1996, Malaysia's manufacturing industries grew so much that they have become the largest part of the economy. In the early 1970s, 70 percent of exports consisted of rubber and tin, but by 1994 manufactured goods accounted for 78 percent of the total value of exports.

Factories in Putrajaya being prepared for new businesses

MAIN SECTORS OF THE ECONOMY	
	(Percentage)
Manufacturing	30
Agriculture	16
Retailing and hotels	12
Financial services	11
Mining	8
Transport and communications	7
Construction	4
Other	12

Sources: *Economist Intelligence Unit Country Profile: Malaysia and Brunei, 1995–96*

Cars at the Proton factory awaiting export to foreign countries

Penang—Silicon Island

Penang, an island off the northwest coast of West Malaysia, is one of the most successful states in the country, but it has been a long, hard struggle. In the 1960s, Penang was in the thick of a depression, with 16 percent of its working population unemployed. The local authority tried to attract companies from overseas, whose businesses would employ a large number of people. By the 1990s, unemployment had dropped to below 5 percent, but most of the workers had few skills and were poorly paid.

Unhappy with this situation, Penang has made itself into a high-tech industrial center based on electronics. At first it developed electrical assembly plants, but now Penang is basing its future on the production of computer disk drives. Both Hewlett-Packard and Intel are among the increasing number of multinational computer companies that have based themselves on the island. Others have relocated on the mainland opposite Penang, which is joined to it by the longest road bridge in Asia—the Penang Bridge. A huge number of local companies are now established in landscaped industrial parks and provide components to multinational companies.

Many of the factory units are still assembly and finishing plants for Japanese and American components, but this is changing. With help from the Penang Skills Development

"My original home is in Sarawak. I'm from the Iban ethnic group, but I have been sent to West Malaysia to receive training from an American company, which is going to build a new factory near my hometown. This is a great opportunity for me because I am receiving real, on-the-job experience. With these new skills I really feel that I can move forward in the future. Expectations are high in this industry, and we really have to do our best."
—Edward Philip Ak Aga, computer disk technician, age 23

Corporation, local workers are now involved in research, development, and processing and are taking the place of foreign workers.

Penang's infrastructure unfortunately lags behind the growth of high-tech production. There are regular power cuts in Penang, and the road network, although improved, is inadequate. Soaring labor costs might also lead the multinational companies to look for another Asian base, where workers are paid less. Despite these disadvantages, there remains a booming economy in Penang.

As financial services expand, banks in Malaysia will become a more common sight.

Malaysia's economic growth is due to the improvement of traditional areas of industry, such as rubber production, and the development of new industries such as electronics. For example, Malaysia has become the world's biggest producer of computer disk drives. National industries, producing goods for the people of Malaysia, have also expanded and now sell their products abroad. Proton, the national car, for instance, is as popular overseas as it is in Malaysia.

However, there is a shortage of skilled labor as the economy grows faster than it can train its workers. In the future, school education needs to be improved. Schools will have to prepare students for the type of work that they are now more likely to find. There is also a shortage of manual workers because of the rapid pace of development.

Furthermore, most manufacturing exports are products made for foreign multinational companies, so the profits from such exports are rarely invested back into Malaysia's economy. However, it is hoped that, as Malaysia develops further, these problems will be overcome.

FINANCE

Malaysia's government has set out to make Kuala Lumpur one of the world's leading financial centers. Kuala Lumpur has been trying to "steal" business from Hong Kong before the Chinese take control of the island in 1997. Some banks in Kuala Lumpur have already agreed to relocate.

Malaysia has also begun a program of privatization. The sale of public assets raises money for the government and helps to pay for development.

There are more new jobs in Malaysia than there are people to fill them. Skilled labor is in short supply, but the government is taking steps to change this situation. University study has been shortened from four to three years to enable trained people to start work earlier. The problems became worse because the government recommended that *Bahasa Melayu*, the official language, should be the only language used in education. *Bahasa* does not lend itself easily to science instruction, so most Malay students study arts subjects.

The Chinese, on the other hand, tend to travel abroad and many are taught in English. When they come back to Malaysia, they are qualified to take the more technical jobs. The policy favoring the use of *Bahasa Melayu* has somewhat backfired, and calls to revive English as a common education language have been heard.

The flow of students to foreign universities poses another problem for Malaysia. It is estimated that there are 50,000 Malaysian students studying overseas at any one time. There is a risk that these students will not come back to work in Malaysia, and, even while they are abroad, their money will be spent in the country of study rather than at home. One way of stopping this drain is to bring foreign education to Malaysia, thus encouraging students to stay. London University in Great Britain is currently involved in talks to set up a campus in Malaysia.

CONSTRUCTION

The amount of construction being carried out in Malaysia becomes clear as you fly into Kuala Lumpur. There are hundreds of new, low-cost and high-cost housing developments in the western area. Suburban and new town development is matched by the Kuala Lumpur city center project. Here the world's tallest office building, the Petronas Tower, is being built.

Cement is in short supply in Malaysia. A builder carefully protects his ration.

34

The pace of development has been greater than expected. As new houses have been erected quickly, standards have fallen. Some, which fail the rigorous building regulations, have never been occupied. The constant building work has also resulted in a cement shortage in Malaysia, and supplies and prices are now strictly controlled to keep it from running out. Major government projects take priority, so some smaller projects have come to a complete halt.

Trash litters an open sewer in Kuala Lumpur.

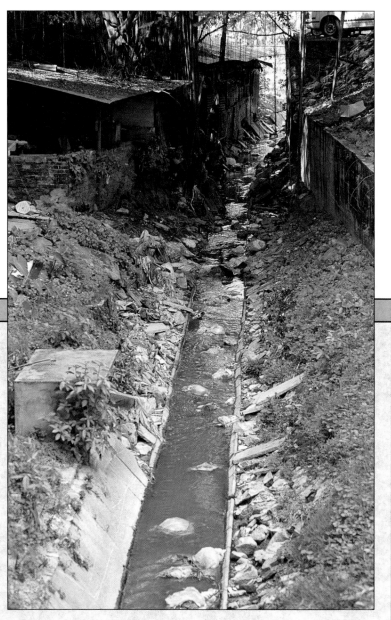

POLLUTION IN KUALA LUMPUR

As the number of factories in Malaysia grows, the levels of pollution and waste increase. The people of Kuala Lumpur were once proud that their city was not like Bangkok, which is well known for its congested streets and poor air quality. Unfortunately, this is no longer the case.

In 1994, massive fires on the Indonesian islands of Sumatra and Kalimantan produced a haze that covered much of Malaysia. It trapped car exhaust and industrial fumes close to ground level. People stayed inside, and schools were threatened with closure. Worse still, the pollution haze descended on Kuala Lumpur again in 1995, only this time there were no Indonesian fires to use as an excuse. Adverse and unusual weather conditions were blamed. Malaysians in the capital care little for the reasons, but deeply regret the loss of blue skies and fresh air. One resident went as far as to say that if this was what development brought, she would rather do without it.

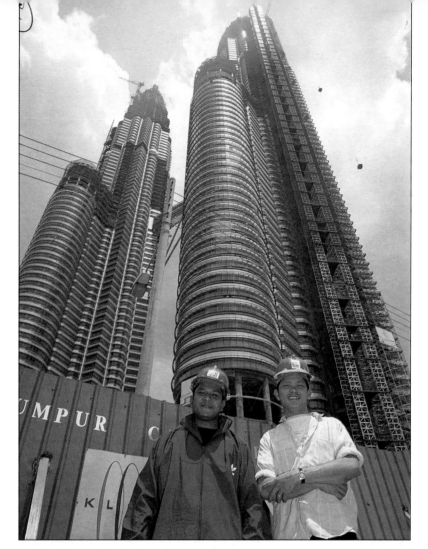

Construction workers in front of the Petronas Tower, the tallest building in the world

"We are very proud to be involved in this great project. It is a big change for an Asian country to have the tallest building in the world. Wouldn't you be proud? We work with other Asian partners. The Japanese are helping us with one of the towers and the other is being built by the South Koreans. They have got the technology to do this, but then we will have it soon."—**Mr. Ifmail and Mr. Mohamad, construction workers at KLCC**

THE PROTON CAR

Perusahaan Otomobil Nasional, or Proton, is a car that first appeared in 1985 in a joint project with the Japanese car manufacturer Mitsubishi. In just ten years, Proton already controls more than 70 percent of the domestic car market. This is partly because high import duties on foreign cars make Protons cheaper, but this no-nonsense car has also been successful overseas. In 1993, more than 17,000 Protons were exported to Great Britain.

The project has also developed local engineering skills. From the very beginning, the number of foreign parts has been reduced by manufacturing these parts within Malaysia. The success of the "First National Car Project" has led to the second, which will produce the Kancil—a cheaper model than the Proton.

Assembling cars in the Proton factory

Key

- 🏭 Oil and gas fields
- ⛴ Ports
- ▲ Hydroelectric power stations
- —— International cable systems
- —— Domestic cable systems

to Thailand
to Hong Kong
to Philippines
to India

Kuantan
Kuala Lumpur
Johor Bahru
Kuching
Kota Kinabalu

Oil, gas, and hydroelectric power have become vital to Malaysia's economy.

EMPLOYMENT

BY SECTOR	(Percentage)
Service Industries	34.8
Manufacturing	24.8
Agriculture	18.4
Retail Trade	16.7
Transportation	4.8
Mining	0.5

BY OCCUPATION	(Percentage)
Production Workers	34.6
Agricultural Laborers	22
Service Workers	11.2
Sales Workers	10.8
Clerical Workers	10.4
Professional and Technical	8.3
Administration and Management	2.7

Source: *Economist Intelligence Unit Country Profile: Malaysia and Brunei, 1995–96*

A Chinese family shows off its new house, a sign of Malaysia's increasing wealth.

Leisure and Tourism

FOREIGN TRAVEL

You need only to look at the travel shelves in your local bookstore or travel agency to see how important Malaysia is becoming as a tourist destination. It has taken the lead in Southeast Asia for a variety of reasons. Resorts have grown around some of the many beaches, but others are still undeveloped. The mountains and hills, such as the Cameron Highlands, are ideal locations for hiking and activity vacations.

Rain forest parks and nature reserves serve two purposes in Malaysia: They protect the environment, enabling unique and rare species to survive in their natural habitats, and they act as tourist attractions. Sepilok, a sanctuary near Sandakan, where orangutans are reintroduced to the wild after periods in captivity, is one of the most famous examples.

Opposite *Old and new are never far apart in Malaysia. On a beach in Penang modern tourist pursuits take place against a background of traditional boats.*

Below *Modern hotels in Penang cater to wealthy foreign visitors to Malaysia.*

Visitors who want to learn more about the culture of the indigenous groups can stay in longhouses in East Malaysia. Recently, there has also been an increase in international business conventions in Malaysia. This means income not only for the convention center but also for hotels, restaurants, and tourist attractions.

Although it is Malaysia's third-biggest earner of foreign currency, tourism still remains a resource with a great deal of potential growth. The government tried to promote the country internationally with its first "Visit Malaysia Year" in 1990. This was repeated in 1994, and a third is planned, for 1998, when Malaysia hosts the Commonwealth Games.

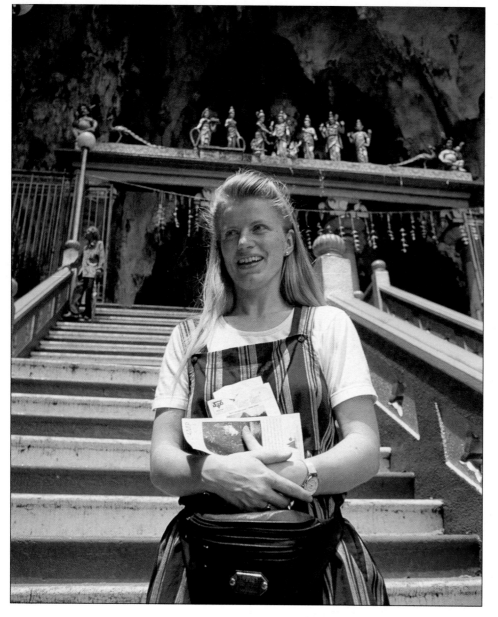

Tourism is important for the Malaysian economy. This tourist explains what she has learned from her visit.

"We are really surprised by the amount of development in Malaysia. We hadn't expected such an organized country. When we told our friends we were going to Malaysia, no one had any idea what it would be like. There seems to be almost no information in Europe about this place, and everybody is so friendly."—Marion Esch, tourist from Germany (left)

In 1993, Orient Express Hotels launched a luxury train service between Singapore and Bangkok. Called the Eastern and Oriental (E&O) Express, it travels the 1,207-mile journey through the Malay Peninsula in forty-two hours. With its wood-paneled interior, inspired by the 1932 movie, *Shanghai Express*, it is aimed more at visitors than locals, although the passengers tend to be a mixture of wealthy Asians and Western honeymoon couples.

Above The Genting Highlands resort is very modern inside and built to suit Western tastes.

Left A family of Indian Malays visits a local zoo for the day.

LOCAL TOURISM

As the Malaysian people have moved from the countryside to towns, their traditions have changed. Through better jobs, they now have more spare time and more money. This means that more Malaysians can now afford to take vacations. Local tourism has seen old hill stations, such as the Genting Highlands, converted into resorts that offer expensive hotels, golf courses, casinos, and karaoke bars. Many Malaysians have no wish to leave their home comforts behind, so the resorts have recreated the luxuries of the city in the countryside.

LEISURE

Among young people, video games are popular, as are American movies, which often appear many months before they are shown in Europe. Hamburger bars are places for the young to meet and relax. However, leisure time is often quite organized. Young Malaysians are encouraged to belong to groups and clubs, such as the Rakan Muda, which provide opportunities to experience the many outdoor activities of this beautiful country.

The one obsession that unites all of the population is badminton. Malaysians are among the best in the world at this sport, and they are looking forward to winning medals when the Commonwealth Games are held in their country in 1998.

UNCLE TAN

Although tourism in eastern Sabah is still not well established, local business people are realizing its potential and are claiming exclusive rights to many places of interest. Resorts that are built to cater entirely to rich overseas visitors are too expensive for locals and budget travelers. The island of Sipidan, which is considered one of the best scuba diving sites in the world, is an example.

Uncle Tan runs a guest house outside Sandakan. He still offers the chance to visit the offshore Turtle Islands quite cheaply, or spend time in a basic jungle camp, living among the proboscis monkeys. But even Uncle Tan is finding it difficult to compete. The policy to encourage a more expensive type of tourism does not benefit the local economy as other types might. Besides, locals feel angry at not being able to afford to visit sights that were once open to all.

"All tourists are different and expect a different approach to tourism facilities, but everybody wants to experience the real Sabah. We have to balance between all the demands on our environment, from industry through to tourism. We can all survive together, but if we let our environment be ruined, it will affect us all. Making quick money will benefit no one. It is the long-term strategy that is vital."

—Uncle Tan, small guest house owner

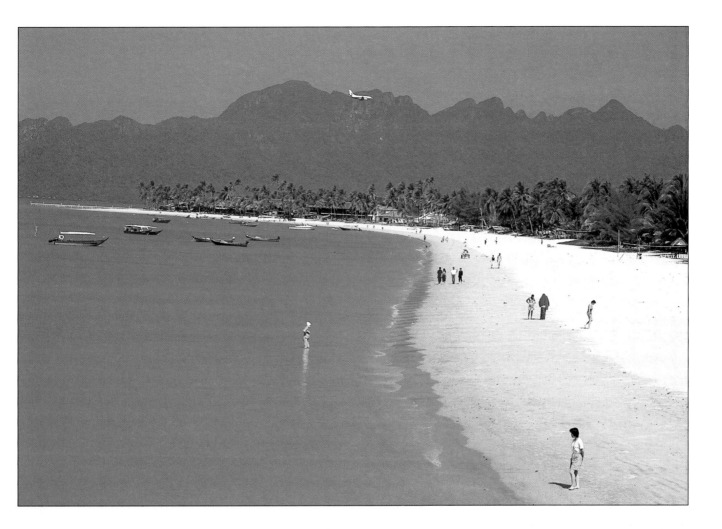

One of the more popular tourist destinations in Lankawi, to the northwest of the peninsula.

PULAU LABUAN

Pulau Labuan, situated 6 miles west of Sabah in the South China Sea, is a strange place. It marks the point where tourism and economic development meet. Although it does not appear to be either tourist island or international offshore financial center, it is both. The biggest attraction is its duty-free shopping. People from Brunei, a nearby Islamic country, come to buy alcohol, which is banned in their country. Yet the island largely consists of buildings that are just two to four stories high, with only limited international standard accommodations.

Nightlife is confined to a few pubs, dance clubs, and karaoke bars.

There are only two real tourist attractions —a Japanese war memorial that marks the point where Japanese forces surrendered at the end of World War II, and the Chimney, which stands as a lasting memory of early industry based on coal. But all might change if the Malaysian government has its way. An exclusive "financial park" is currently being built, and it is hoped that it will turn the island into an offshore banking resort to rival Singapore and Hong Kong.

The Future— "Vision 2020"

The future of Malaysia looks bright. It has one of the fastest-growing economies of any Asian country. To keep this growth on target, Prime Minister Dr. Mahathir Mohammed has introduced a strategic plan called "Vision 2020." It is a plan that aims for full industrialization by the year 2020. Everywhere you go in Malaysia the idea is highlighted with banners and posters, displayed on bridges and flower displays.

In April 1995, Dr. Mahathir won the general election with more votes than ever. The prime minister is very popular. On National Day (*Merdeka*) or other special occasions, full-page advertisements in the newspapers praise him as a champion of the Third World.

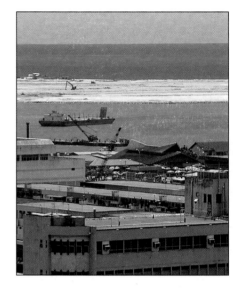

Above Extra land for development has been reclaimed from the sea in Kota Kinabalu.

AT HOME

This support allows the prime minister to press ahead with his grand plans. Having built the world's tallest flagpole in the capital, Kuala Lumpur, Dr. Mahathir has his sights set on finishing the world's tallest building.

The forests are being cleared to build the world's tallest hydroelectric dam, at Bakun; a new airport is taking shape at Sepang, and the sports complex that will host the Commonwealth Games will be finished by 1998.

The largest and most ambitious plan will give Malaysia a new capital city. Called Putrajaya, and located 25 miles south of Kuala Lumpur, the city will form a triangle with the new airport and current capital. Putrajaya will be a new "mega-city," based on satellite and multimedia technology.

An advertisement for the new airport at Sepang

As development is not cheap, the government has cut costs by privatizing the main projects. For example, private companies have built the north–south highway and now charge a toll for vehicles on certain sections.

ABROAD

Dr. Mahathir is gaining more respect from other world leaders. While the prime minister might appear quick to respond to criticism, he knows that Malaysia is now so important that it cannot be ignored.

The health of the financial center appears to be strong. Banks are becoming nervous about the Chinese taking control in Hong Kong in 1997, and some will look for another Southeast Asian capital in which to relocate. Some have already mentioned that they favor Kuala Lumpur. In 1996, the Kuala Lumpur Stock Exchange (KLSE) will become fully automated, which is bound to increase the activity on its market.

Architects have the best view of what the future will look like in Malaysia. They are perhaps the most important people in the prime minister's "Vision 2020."

FURTHER DEVELOPMENT

According to Dr. Mahathir, "Malaysia is developing so rapidly that it has been recognized by international organizations as a model for developing countries." But has the development been too fast? If labor wages keep rising, the Malaysians might price themselves out of the market. Foreign companies will then look for similar countries where both labor and land is cheaper. It is therefore essential that Malaysia carefully manage its further development in order to maintain its enormous success.

Glossary

Canopy The highest leafy layer in the rain forests.

Cash crops Crops that are produced for sale and not for personal use.

Colonial Of a country occupied and ruled by another country.

Commodity Something that is produced using human labor.

Congestion Traffic caused by busy roads.

Deforestation A reduction in the area of land covered by trees.

Dialects Forms of a language that belong to specific groups of people.

Erosion Wearing away of the land by natural agents such as wind or waves.

Ethnic Having to do with groups of people as based on their culture, etc.

Exploit To make the maximum use of a resource.

Exports Products that a country sells abroad.

Humidity The degree of moisture in the air.

Hydroelectric power Electric power that is produced by the energy of water.

Immigrants People who choose to move from their home country to another country.

Indigenous Originating naturally in a particular area (plants and wildlife) or being native to a particular region (people).

Industrialization The growth of large industries based on machines.

Infrastructure The system of public works of a country, such as transportation and communications.

Integration The successful mixing of an ethnic group into a society.

Manufacturing Making raw products into materials that can be sold.

Monarchy A state ruled by a king or a queen.

Primary production Industrial activity concerned with collecting or producing material that is natural, i.e., agriculture or mining.

Privatization The changing of a business or industry from public control to private ownership.

Reclaimed land Areas of land that were once under water that have been taken back from the sea.

Resource Wealth supplied by nature, such as energy, minerals, or lumber.

Shifting cultivation A process by which land is cleared, cropped, and then abandoned for another piece when the soil becomes exhausted.

Stock Exchange A trading place where people meet to buy and sell shares in different companies.

Sustainable Able to be maintained without reducing future levels.

Tropical Very hot and wet climate.

Urbanization A process involving the change of any area from countryside into towns.

Further Information

Malaysian Embassy, 2401 Massachusetts Avenue, Washington, D.C. 20008

Both the *Lonely Planet Travel Survival Kit* and *Rough Guide* travel guides include lengthy descriptions of Malaysia and its people.

The Star, an English-language newspaper in Malaysia reprints important stories on a World Wide Web page which is updated daily (http://www.jaring.my/%7Estar/).

Books to read

Lambert, David. *Asia*. Continents. Austin, TX: Raintree Steck-Vaughn, 1996.

Lerner Publications, Department of Geography Staff, ed. *Malaysia in Pictures*. Visual Geography. Minneapolis, MN: Lerner Group, 1989.

Mason, Anthony. *Southeast Asia*. World in View. Austin, TX: Raintree Steck-Vaughn, 1992.

Munan, Heidi. *Malaysia*. Cultures of the World. Bellmore, NY: Marshall Cavendish, 1991.

Rigg, Jonathan. *Southeast Asia*. Country Fact Files. Austin, TX: Raintree Steck-Vaughn, 1995.

Wright, David K. *Malaysia*. Enchantment of the World. Chicago: Children's Press, 1988.

Index

Numbers in **bold** refer to illustrations.